PAPER TRICKS

by Florence Temko

Drawings by Linda Winchester

SCHOLASTIC INC.
New York Toronto London Auckland Sydney

HELPFUL HINTS

WHEN YOU SEE THIS:	IT MEANS:
Solid Line	Cut
Dotted Line	Fold UP (makes a valley)
Broken Line	Fold BACK (makes a mountain)
Arrow	Fold in this direction
Rolled Arrow	Turn paper over
Fold	Crease sharply

Read all the way through the instructions before you begin a project. If you want to make more than one copy of any of the projects, trace the pattern on another piece of paper before you cut it out.

ISBN   0–590–41129–2

13

RUBBER PAPER

Would you believe you can put your head through this piece of paper? Here's how:

1. Cut out the square.
2. Fold paper in half on the broken line.
3. Cut along the solid lines through both layers of paper. Some cuts begin at the folded edge, some at the open edges. Do not cut all the way across.
4. Open the paper flat. Cut on the broken line between the two X's. Gently s-t-r-e-t-c-h the ends of the paper to make a big circle. This is a great trick to try out on your friends.

See back of page.

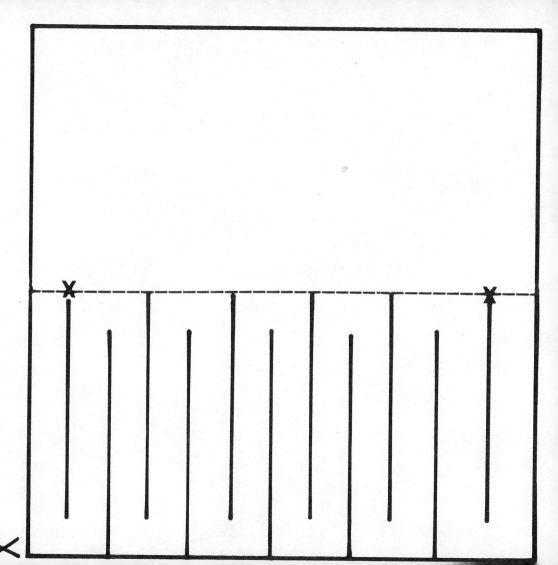

Cut out a bigger piece of rubber paper you can step through.

SPY PLANE

1. Cut out the square.
2. Fold BACK on broken lines 1 to 5.
3. Fold UP on dotted line 6.
4. Loosen the wings. Slip a paperclip cn the body near the nose to make the plane fly better.

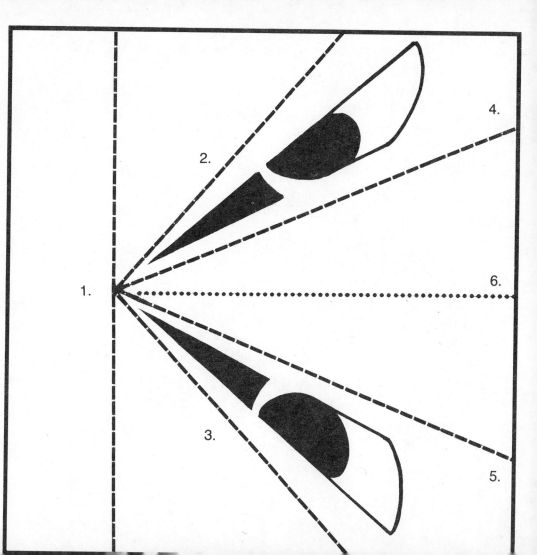

SECRET MESSAGE

You need a piece of notebook paper.

1. Write your message on one side of the paper. Fold paper in half lengthwise with message inside.
2. Fold paper in half again.
3. Fold a triangle at one end.
4. Keep folding the paper over in triangles.
5. Tuck the end flap neatly into the "pocket."

See back of page.

Suggestion

You can play a game of football with a piece of paper folded like the SECRET MESSAGE. Stand the folded triangle on a point. Two players take turns flicking the triangle back and forth. Make up your own scoring rules. Form goalposts with your hands.

SKELETON FISH

1. Cut out the square.
2. Fold on the broken line.
3. Cut out the fish on the solid line through both layers of paper.
4. Cut on the solid lines. Some cuts start at the folded edges. Some start on the rounded edge. Do not cut all the way across.
5. Open the paper flat. Hold the head and tail and s-t-r-e-t-c-h the paper.

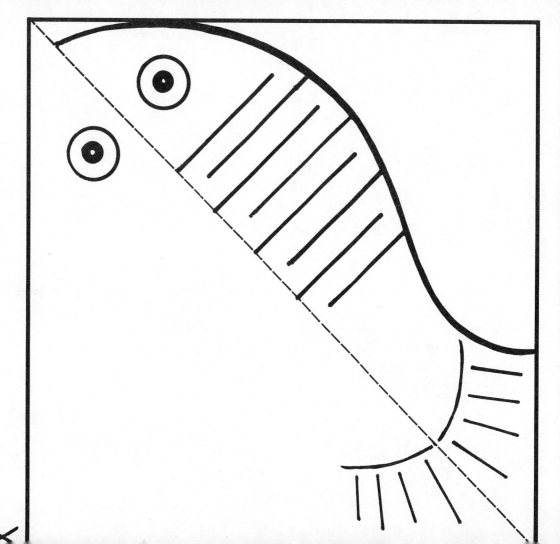

ORIGAMI BIRD

Origami birds make great favors for parties. Make them out of white paper and decorate them. Or make them out of giftwrap paper.

1. Cut out the square. Fold the outer edges to the middle on the dotted lines.

More instructions on next page.

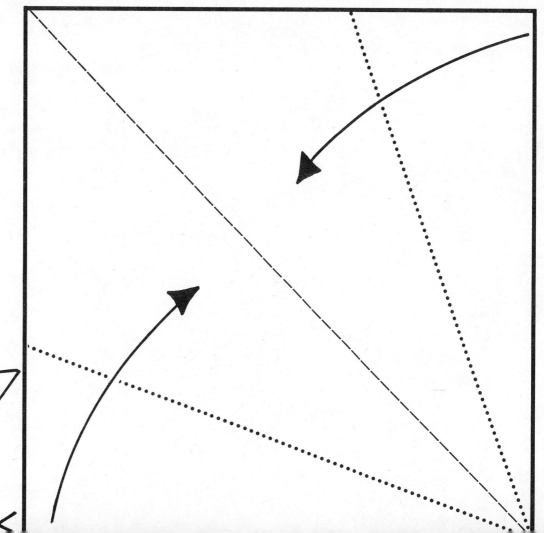

ORIGAMI BIRD
CONTINUED

2. Fold the bottom corner to the top corner.
3. Fold the tip down.
4. Fold BACK on the broken line.
5. Pull the beak out and then the neck will move up at the same time.
6. Crease the paper sharply at the X's to make the neck and head stay in place. Fold the feet to the side.

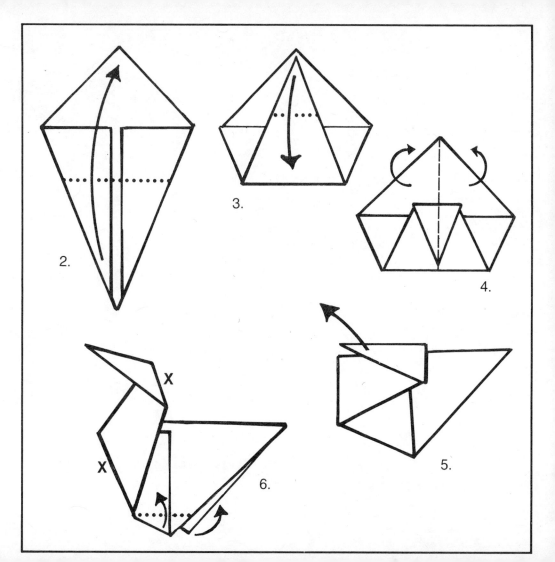

EARRINGS

1. Cut out the four small squares and color each one.
2. Fold BACK on the three broken lines.
3. Overlap triangles A and B and glue them together.
4. Pierce a hole at the top. Insert enough thread to make large loops to hang around your ears. You can also buy earring fittings in hobby and craft stores.

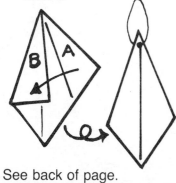

See back of page.

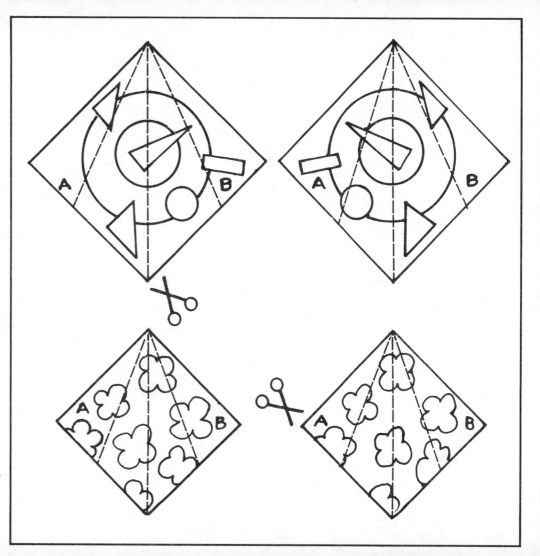

Suggestion

You can use small squares of foil giftwrap paper to make earrings that look like real jewelry.

FRIENDSHIP BRACELET

1. Cut out the square. Color all over one side of the paper.
2. Fan-pleat the paper by folding back and forth on the lines.
3. Flatten the longest crease.
4. Roll the strip into a circle. Put the bracelet on your arm. Slide one end into the other.

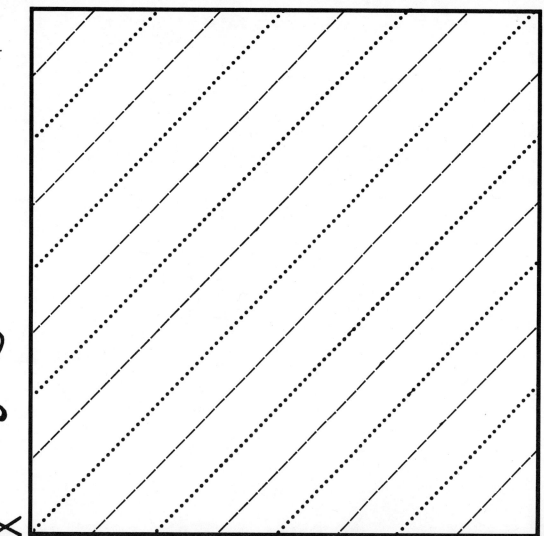

See back of page.

Suggestion

You can pleat bigger friendship bracelets with larger paper squares. Try gold or silver gift-wrap paper.

3-D STAR

1. Color the star any way you like.
2. Cut out the star.
3. Fold UP on the dotted lines. Unfold after each crease.
4. Fold BACK on the broken lines. Unfold after each crease.
5. Make sure the creases go up and down in turn. Now you have a 3-D star.

See back of page.

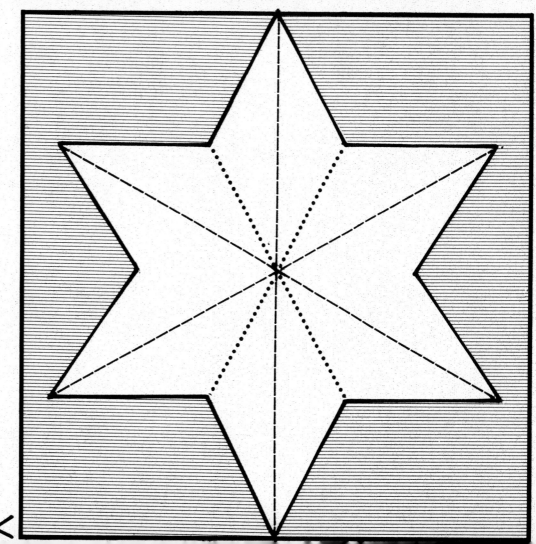

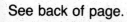

Suggestion

If you want to make more stars, trace the outline of your star onto other pieces of paper. Use silver or other colored paper to make holiday stars.

SOMERSAULT SALLY

You will need an index card, 3 inches by 5 inches.

1. Fold the card in half, lengthwise. Unfold. Fold the two top corners to the middle crease. Fold the bottom edge up about ½ inch.
2. Fold both side edges to the middle crease.
3. Fold UP the bottom edge along the dotted line, as shown.
4. Fold in half, as shown.
5. Set up Sally and tap her on the back. She'll somersault. You can draw on a funny face.

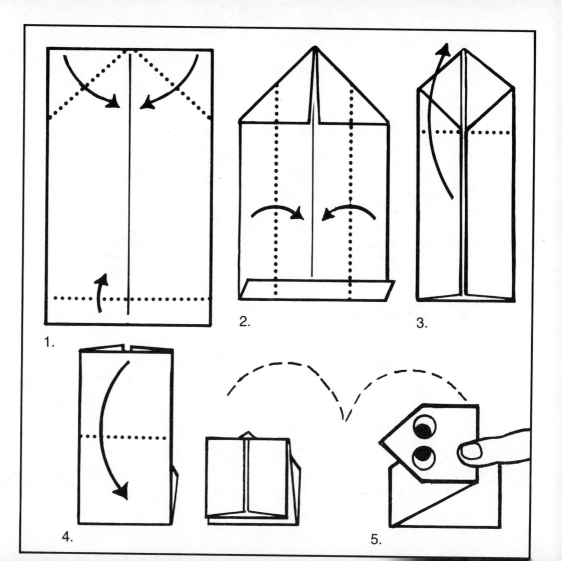

VALENTINE

1. Color the right arch red.
2. Cut out the two arches. Cut slits in each arch on the solid lines.
3. Place the white section on top of the red section to make a heart shape.
4. Weave the white strips through the red strips to get the checkerboard look in the drawing.
5. Line up the edges. Use a small drop of glue at the ends to hold the strips together.

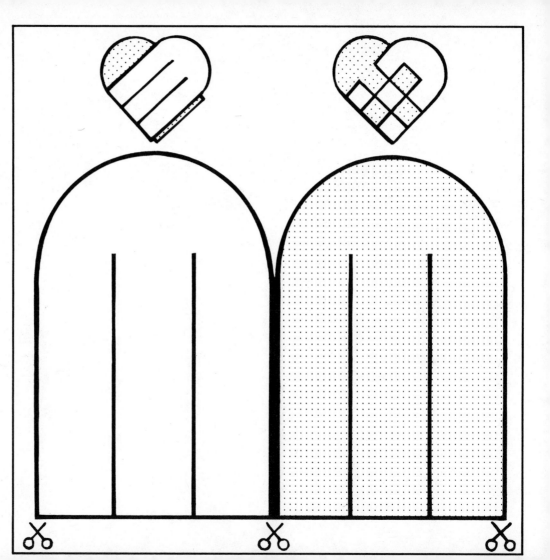

See back of page.

Suggestion

You can write messages on tiny pieces of paper and hide them in the valentine.

CHICKEN POP-UP

1. Cut out the pop-up.
2. Fold in half so the face is on the outside. Cut the beak on the solid line. Fold back and forth on the dotted lines.
3. Fold the paper so the face is hidden inside. Open the paper a little and push the beak to the inside.

Now when you open and shut the paper, the beak will pop open.

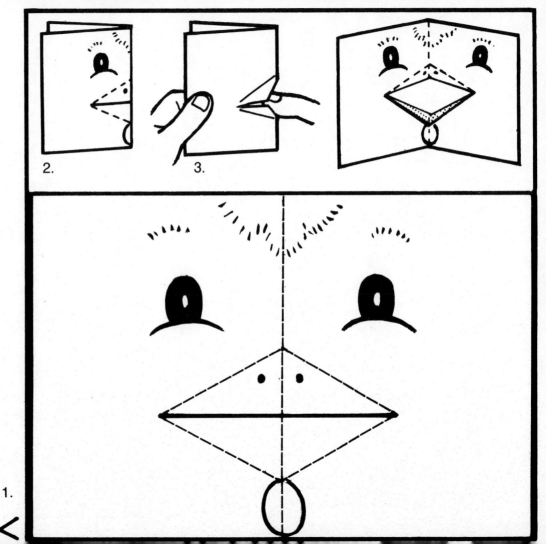

See back of page.

Suggestion

You can use the pop-up for a greeting card. Color it. Paste the four corners of the pop-up inside a piece of folded construction paper.

HOLIDAY ORNAMENT

1. Cut out the orna-
   ment on the solid
   line.
2. Color the designs.
3. Glue all four tips on
   top of each other.
4. Thread a string
   through the top or
   use an ornament
   hanger.

See back of page.

Cut more ornaments from other pieces of paper. Color them or paste on designs. Silver giftwrap paper makes the ornaments look like spacecraft. Combine several into a mobile.

POPCORN PYRAMID

1. Cut on the solid lines. Color the popcorn and the background.
2. Fold BACK on all the broken lines.
3. Glue the tabs on the inside.
4. Attach a thread or ornament hanger.

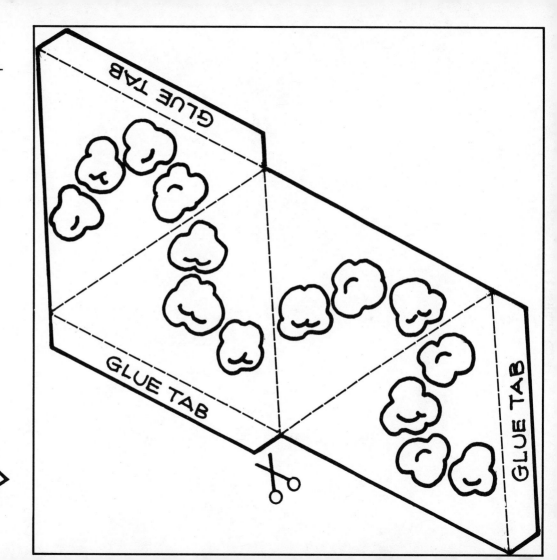

DOLLAR-BILL RING

Make a ring from a dollar bill or use a plain piece of paper of the same size, 6 inches by 2½ inches. At each step be sure the bill is placed exactly as shown in the drawings.

1. Put down the bill with the picture of Washington facing up, but upside down. Fold UP the white edges at the top and bottom. Fold the bill in half from bottom to top.
2. Fold the top to the bottom.
3. Fold BACK on the broken lines exactly in the three places shown.

See back of page.

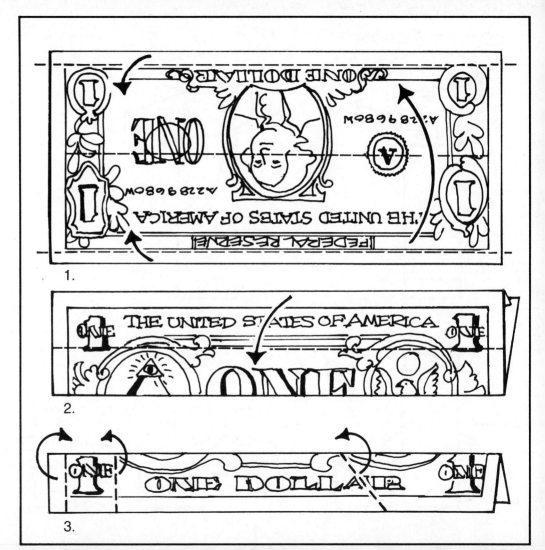

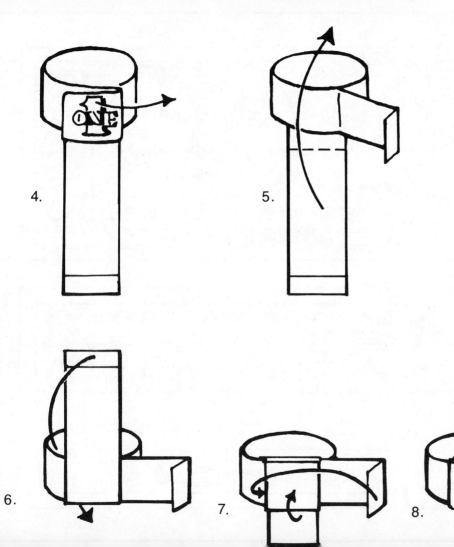

4. Roll the strip into a ring, so that the end with the "1" is on top of the end with the "tail."
5. Flip the "1" end out of the way to the right.
   Fold the tail up.
6. Fold the tail down inside the ring.
7. Fold UP the short leftover piece of the tail as tightly as possible.
8. To lock the ring, bring the "1" end over and tuck the white edge into the "pocket." You may need to push it in with the points of a scissors.

ORIGAMI BALL

1. Cut out the square. Fold UP on the dotted lines. Unfold. Fold BACK on the broken lines. Leave paper folded on one of the broken lines. You'll have a triangle.

More instructions on next page.

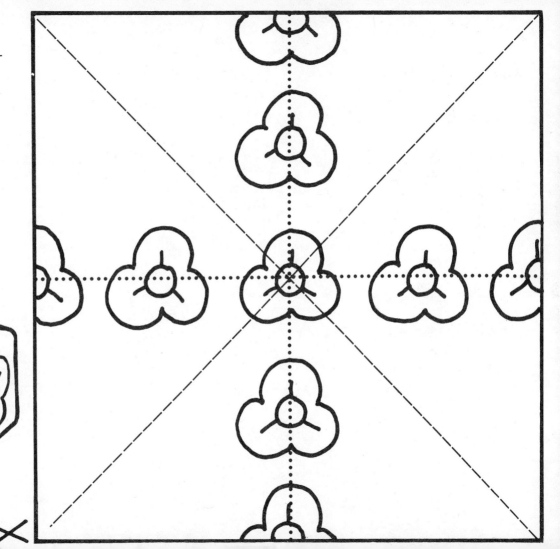

2. Hold the paper as shown. Push the sides together until you have a smaller triangle. Put down the triangle with two flaps on each side.

3. Fold UP the outer corners of the top flaps. Turn paper over and do the same on the back.

4. Fold the side corners of the top flaps to the middle. Turn paper over and do the same on the back.

5. Tuck the loose tips at the top into the pockets of the triangles as far as you can. Repeat on the back.

6. To blow up: Hold the ball between your fingers and thumbs. Put the open end to your mouth. Blow in the opening.

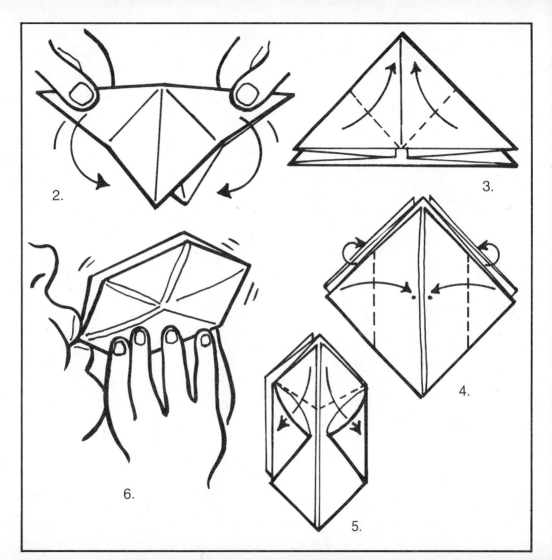

STUNT PLANE

You need a piece of paper 8½ inches by 11 inches.

1. Fold the paper in half lengthwise. Unfold. Fold two corners to the middle crease.
2. Fold the triangle over.
3. Make a dot 1 inch up from the tip of the triangle. Fold the outside corners of the triangle to the dot.
4. Fold UP the tip.
5. Fold the slanted edges to the middle.

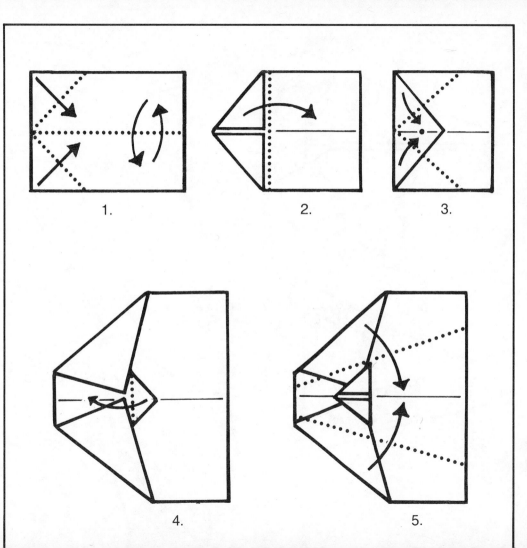

1.

2.

3.

4.

5.

See back of page

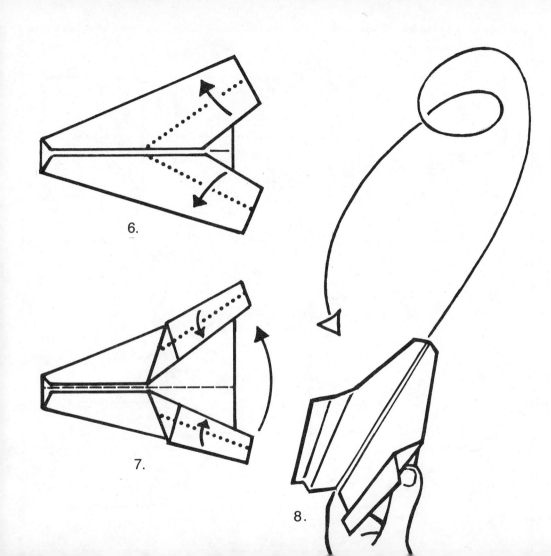

6.

7.

8.

6. Fold the back wings along dotted lines as shown in the drawing.
7. Pleat the back wings by folding them in half along dotted lines. Then fold the plane in half lengthwise with the wings on the outside.
8. Spread the wings away from the plane and loosen the pleats at the back. Launch the plane with its nose up in the air. It will loop. You can staple the plane together underneath.

PETE
THE PENGUIN

1. Cut out the square.
2. Fold BACK on lines 1 to 4.
3. Fold UP on line 5.
4. Pull out the nose until you can crease the back of the head on line 6.

Stand the penguin upright.

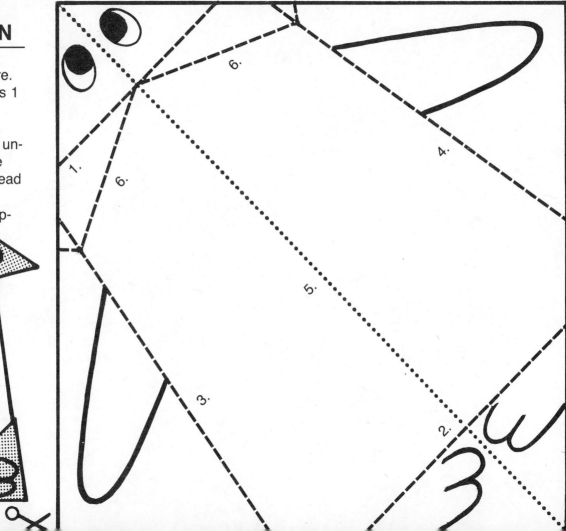

MYSTERY CUTOUT

1. Cut out the square. Fold BACK on the broken line. Now you can read the mystery word.
2. Carefully cut around the letters, through both layers of paper. Be sure to leave the letters connected at the fold.
3. Unfold. Paste the cut-out on a piece of construction paper. It will look like a tree.

See back of page.

Suggestion

You can design your own mystery cutout. With a wide felt-tip pen, write a word or name on a folded piece of paper. Make sure all letters touch the fold. Then cut out. You can use mystery cutouts to make greeting cards.

ALLY ALLOSAURUS

1. Cut out the square.
2. Fold BACK on the broken line.
3. Cut out Ally through both layers of paper.
4. Cut on short solid lines on back. Fold back small triangles to make scales.
5. Color Ally any way you like.

Try to design other stand-up animals.

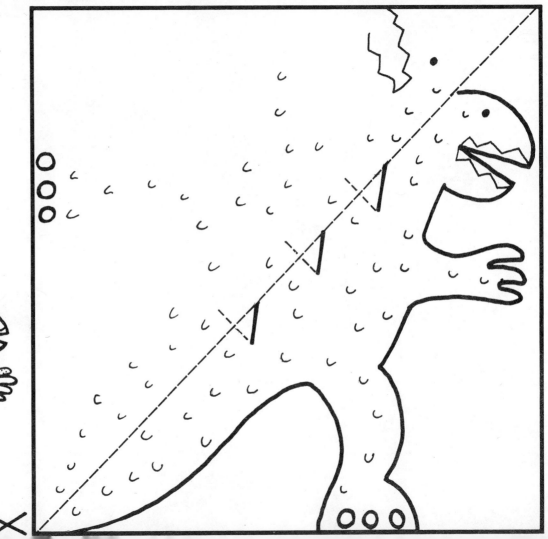

TREASURE BOX

Once this box is closed it can only be opened by tearing it — unless you know the secret.

1. Cut out the box on all the solid lines.
2. Carefully cut slits in corners A and B.
3. Fold BACK on all the broken lines.

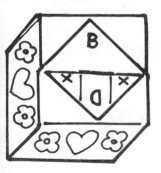

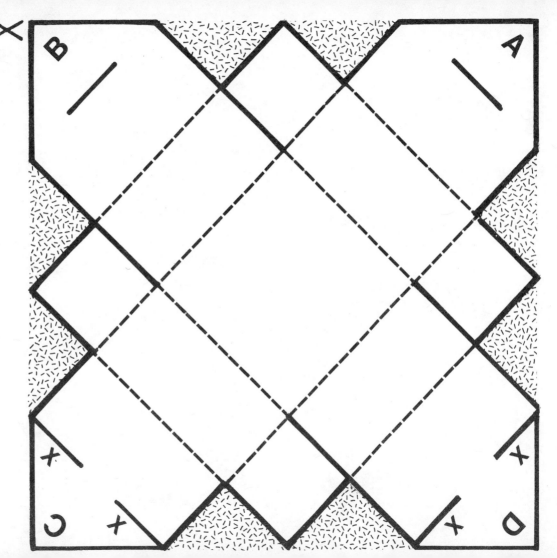

See back of page.

4. Overlap the two X's on corner C. Do not make sharp creases. Now you can slide corner C into slot A. Spread the flap so the two X's show again. Repeat with corner D, sliding it into slot B.

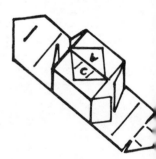

PUZZLE CUBE

The Puzzle: to make a cube from three paper rings.

1. Cut on all the solid lines. You will have three strips.
2. Fold on the broken lines so that the dots are on the outside.
3. Glue strips A and C into square rings.
4. Loop strip B through the other two rings. Glue the ends of this strip together.

Can you shape the three rings into a cube without making any new folds? When you know how to do it, challenge a friend.

Solution on back of page.

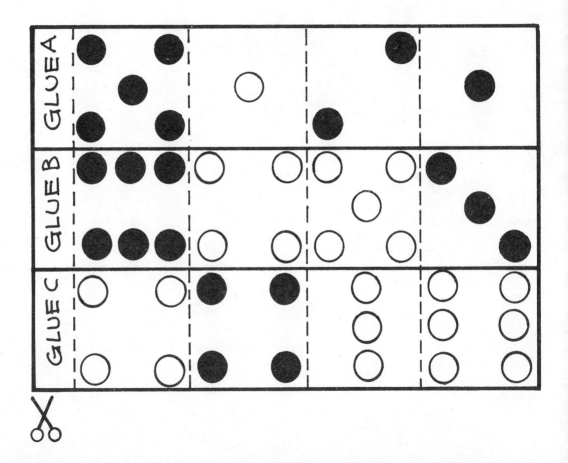

Solution for Puzzle Cube. Swing left ring A to the front of middle ring B. Push them into each other. Push ring C to the left.

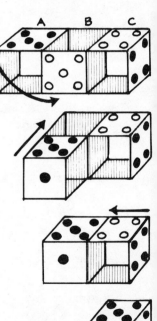